COMPACT HOUSES

COMPACT HOUSES

Cristina del Valle

Universe

Editor: Nacho Asensio

Editorial coordination and text: Cristina del Valle Schuster

Translation: Michael Brunelle

Graphic design: Núria Sordé

Layout: M.ª José Jiménez

First published in the United States of America in 2005 by
Universe Publishing
A Division of Rizzoli International Publications, Inc.
300 Park Avenue South
New York, NY 10010
www.rizzoliusa.com

2005 © Bookslab S.L.

2005 2006 2007 2008 / 10 9 8 7 6 5 4 3 2 1

ISBN 0-7893-1349-9

Library of Congress Control Number 2005903671

Printed in Spain by Anman Gràfiques del Vallès

CONTENTS

10
SLIT VILLA

18
LAYER HOUSE

26
TAVOLA

32
PIXEL HOUSE

40
NATURAL WEDGE

48
WHITE RIBBING

56
FOLD HOUSE

64
ROOFTECTURE M

72
HAUS P

80
018

88
HOUSE IN
SETAGAYA

94
ELLIOTT HOUSE

102
THE LONG HOUSE

110
HOUSE IN
MOTOAZABU

118
KASSAI HOUSE

128
M7 PROTOTYPE

136
COCOON HOUSE

146
CLAUDIA
BRUCKNER
RESIDENCE

154
MINIMAL HOUSE

162
A HOUSE
IN THE GARDEN

170
SOL

176
RUPP HOUSE

184
SINGLE-FAMILY
HOME IN GAUSES

192
WESTLAKE HOUSE

200
OPEN
TO THE RIVER

210
MISONOU HOUSE

218
4x4 HOUSE

226
SINGLE-FAMILY
HOUSE AND STUDIO

236
HOUSE IN
VANDOEUVRES

244
REBUILDING
OF HOUSE KÖNIG

250
DONG HEON
RESIDENCE

258
2PARTS HOUSE

266
SOLAR BOX

274
LEVIS HOUSE

282
BETIKOA

290
ZENZMAIER
HOUSE

298
STUDIO AND
GUESTHOUSE
GROSSENSEE

308
ZIG ZAG CABIN

316
WEE HOUSE

324
BOATHOUSE

332
SUMMER
CONTAINER

338
BOX HOUSE

346
KEENAN TOWER
HOUSE

354
SNOWBOARDERS
COTTAGE

362
CLARABOYA
HOUSE

370
HOLIDAY HOME
SEEWALD

378
SUMMERHOUSE IN
DYNGBY

386
M HOUSE

394
SUMMER HOUSE

400
HOUSE AT
JUQUEHY

408
HOUSE IN
CARRASCAL

INTRODUCTION

Throughout history the way people constructed their dwellings reflected their view of themselves and their standing in the world in which they lived. Unlike the old days, when a person's social status was measured by owning a house that was as large as his pockets were deep, in modern times we are seeing a tendency towards smaller scale homes. This type of house includes several encoded values, such as efficiency, cleverness, and sensitivity, which lead to the elimination of all excessive elements in a space that incorporates only the basic functions. Perhaps this is the reason why designers of small houses experiment so freely with architectural parameters. Esthetics and function, materials and forms are combined in a profusion of possible solutions that compete to play a part in this challenge to take advantage of every single inch of space.

"Compact Houses" is a study of over fifty houses, each with no more than 1,300 square feet, that are unique for their versatility and ingenuity, and that offer many clever solutions for designing a compact house. The projects are divided into four chapters, Urban Dwellings, Non-Urban Residences, Additions, and Temporary Retreats, and include works by famous architects such as Tadao Ando, Shuhei Endo, and Marte.Marte Architekten. This is a tour through houses whose small size encourages a high degree of creativity.

URBAN DWELLINGS

The concentrated masses of people in large urban centers have sparked an increased demand for space, and the growing scarcity of available property is causing a considerable increase in the price of housing. This phenomenon has motivated the construction of very small homes that are characterized by their adaptability to lots of all shapes and sizes.

Architects depend on their ingenuity to make the most of the available space, which results in the design of very versatile furnishings. Incorporating different functions in such a small space requires the use of clever tricks, often relying on solutions that fulfill several needs at once, thus maximizing the useable space of the house. Folding tables and convertible beds, seats that have storage space inside, and wide walls that double as storage closets are only a few of the ideas that can be found in the following designs, along with the use of varied structural elements that change the perception of the space and make it look larger than it really is.

SLIT VILLA

In Japan inhabitants and commerce are concentrated in the urban centers, which has caused the well-known lack of space and a growing tendency toward compact residential architecture. Small scale is becoming popular, as illustrated by this house with only 721 square feet located in a densely populated residential area in Tokyo.

The kitchen and dining areas are on the ground floor, while the living area is on the second level. The top floor is reserved for the bedroom and a terrace. A system of rollup and folding bamboo screens cover the facade and create an entertaining and ever changing exterior. The translucent quality of this material, which is also present in the interior, establishes a visual connection between the different spaces of the house and at the same time provides the necessary privacy from the outside. This very sensitive and aesthetic design makes use of traditional materials and presents a modern approach to a solution that combines natural elements with the contemporary spirit of daily life.

721 SQUARE FEET

ARCHITECT
C. MATSUBA/TELE-DESIGN

PHOTOGRAPHER
RYOTA ATARASHI

LOCATION & DATE
TOKYO, JAPAN, 2002

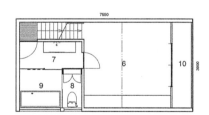

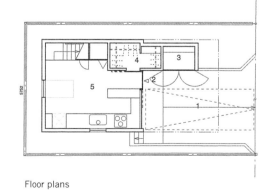

Floor plans

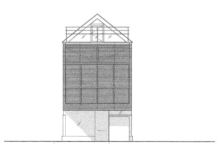

Elevation

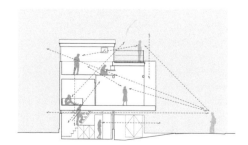

Section

The screens encourage an intimate and comfortable interior. At the same time the material's semi-transparency creates a visual link with the exterior that diminishes the sense of isolation.

A combination of modern and traditional materials such as wood, steel, and bamboo are present throughout the interior, and reflect the contemporary tendency of Japanese architecture.

LAYER HOUSE

This small house occupies just 355 square feet and is located in the center of the city of Kobe. Hiroaki Ohtani, architect and owner of the house, kept a single goal in mind from the beginning: to create the richest and most spacious interior possible, despite the limited dimensions of the building.

The structure is built like a trellis made of horizontal wood boards that alternate with empty spaces between them. The result is a room measuring nine feet four inches wide by twenty-five feet deep.

One of the advantages of this building is that it is, in the words of the architect, "incomplete". Another advantage is the structure's horizontal arrangement, which allows diffused light to flow into the interior.

The rooms are arranged according to the degree of privacy needed for each. The common areas are near the entrance, while the more personal areas are hidden behind them. There are several open areas that serve as connections between the rooms. Floating steps that protrude from the gaps in the trellis-like structure serve as stairways.

355 SQUARE FEET

ARCHITECT
HIROAKI OHTANI

PHOTOGRAPHER
KOUJI OKAMOTO

LOCATION & DATE
KOBE, JAPAN, 2003

Floor plan

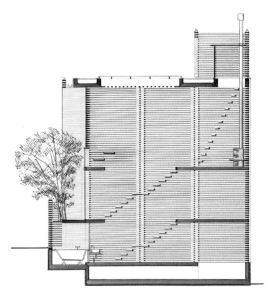

Section

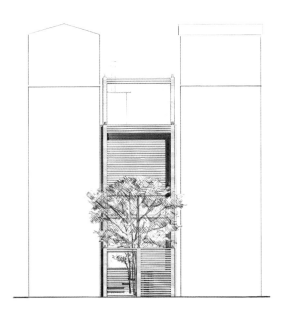

Elevation

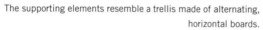

The supporting elements resemble a trellis made of alternating, horizontal boards.

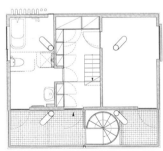

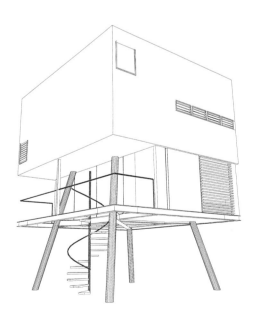

Floor plans

Perspective

The rooms on the top floor were designed leaving out superfluous elements that would hinder the feeling of spaciousness.

PIXEL HOUSE

The Pixel House was designed with a repeating pattern that is reminiscent of the pixels in digital images. The owners, a couple with two children, were interested in a design that would allow them to share part of the exterior with the other residents in the neighborhood.

The house is built on a trapezoidal plan and makes use of a large variety of materials to create an unusual building. The design was made by using sequences of angled bricks to resemble pixels. The bricks also provide a very tangible sense of both the scale and the building process. The result is a house made up of 9,675 pixels (1 pixel = 1 brick).

A semi-private area was created at the back of the house that is directly accessible from the front part of the residence. In fact, any neighbor is invited to come into this space. One of the owners' requirements was to be able to use this setting as a community center during the day and as a private area on nights and weekends.

915 SQUARE FEET

ARCHITECTS
SLADE ARCHITECTURE AND MASS STUDIES

PHOTOGRAPHER
YONG KWAN KIM

LOCATION & DATE
HEIRI, SOUTH KOREA, 2003

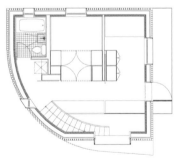

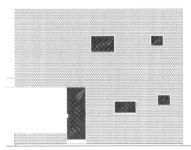

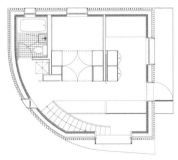

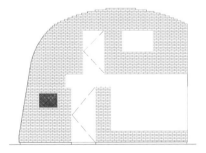

Floor plans

Elevations

34

The result is a house made up of 9,675 bricks that imitate the pixels in a digital image.

The crystal-like structure becomes a magical object when light flows in, making the space come alive.

The interior is open and uninterrupted, integrating the different floors connected by a metal stairway.

WHITE RIBBING

Building a peaceful island in the center of the hectic city of Tokyo is without a doubt a difficult challenge. The Milligram Studio architects met this challenge by creating an irregularly shaped residence built on a rectangular floor plan. The design of the project's facade is free of details. The architecture is strictly formal and based on open spaces and bright interiors. The pentagonal shape encloses a balanced and pure interior where light blends with the white walls to create a feeling of spaciousness. The various rooms are very open and carefully arranged to create a clean and flowing environment.

The irregular structure of the roof gives the top floor a unique, attic-like feeling.

White Ribbing has an expressive strength aspired to by many contemporary single-family homes. This is a striking design with a flexible and flowing interior.

958 SQUARE FEET

ARCHITECTS
MILLIGRAM STUDIO

PHOTOGRAPHER
TAKESHI TAIRA

LOCATION & DATE
TOKYO, JAPAN, 2004

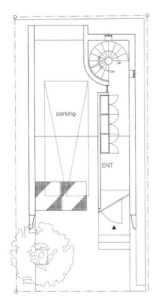

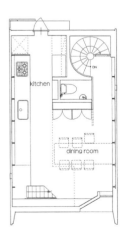

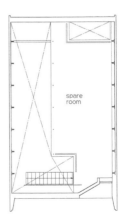

Floor plans

The spaces are flooded with light that is further enhanced by the white walls and ceiling.

FOLD HOUSE

The concept that lends this project coherence came from experimenting with a system of layers based on old Japanese houses constructed from "fusuma" (sliding doors) and "shoji" (paper panels). This residence, located in an industrial area that is experiencing more and more residential construction, explores the architectural potential of using different layers on a structure, as well as the feelings they elicit.

Two partially open and linked frames encourage the flow of nat ural light. The project is defined by its asymmetrical design, exhibited in the shapes of the walls of the two structures, vertical on one side and diagonal on the other, as well as by their surface coverings. Extending this concept, the galvanized steel exterior is smooth while the inside corrugated walls correspond to the smooth outside layer, and in contrast the smooth interior walls reflect a textured exterior surface.

1012 SQUARE FEET

ARCHITECT
MUTSUE HAYAKUSA/CELL SPACE ARCHITECTS

PHOTOGRAPHER
SATOSHI ASAKAWA

LOCATION & DATE
NAGAREYAMA, JAPAN, 2004

Floor plan

Section

Elevation

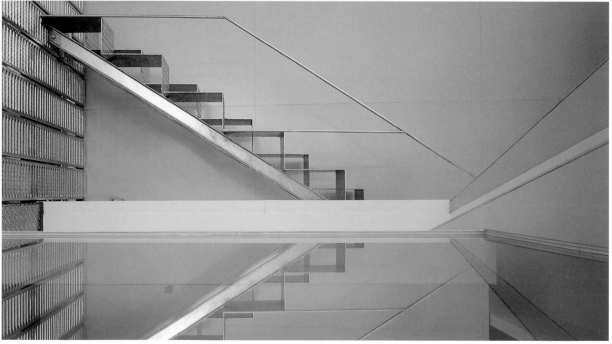

The interior surfaces are somewhat angled to resist horizontal forces as well as seismic movements.

ROOFTECTURE M

The Japanese architect Shuhei Endo pursues coherent paramodern architecture, capable of generating new possibilities and overcoming the limitations of a discipline that is too attached to conformity. Endo experiments with non-compositional methods and rejects spaces that are merely a compilation of lesser elements. In this studio residence, a method called roof-lecture is used to create a single element: continuous metal siding that covers both the roof and the walls instead of separating them into different parts. This is an attempt to create a versatile and continuous residence, a space whose originality stems from the notion of movement.

The two-story dwelling is located on an elongated site. The upper level houses a studio, which has large windows facing the main street while a bathroom and private bedrooms occupy the rest of the floor. The lower level houses common areas.

1023 SQUARE FEET

ARCHITECT
SHUHEI ENDO

PHOTOGRAPHER
YOSHIHARU MATSUMARA

LOCATION & DATE
MARUOKA-CHO, JAPAN, 2001

Floor plan

Sections

Elevation

住いの提案

67

The public and private areas are clearly defined in this unique
residence, an example of the architect's particular style.

住いの提案

HAUS P

The originality of this small residence designed for a family of four, which at first glance seems like one more wood box with a flat roof and large windows, becomes evident after a close look at its details. Ingenious ways of making use of the small spaces can be seen throughout the house, like the small centrally located kitchen that is installed in a wood cabinet and can be closed and kept out of sight.

Each one of the rooms has at least one glass wall, which creates a visual connection between them and conveys the sense of light and space required to overcome the cramped feeling typical of small spaces. This is all possible thanks to an interior patio that directs sunlight into the central parts of the house, which would otherwise receive much less light than the outside rooms. This opening also creates a sense of space, creating the illusion of a much larger area.

1076 SQUARE FEET

ARCHITECTS
THALER. THALER ARCHITEKTEN

PHOTOGRAPHER
HR. SINA BANIAHMAD

LOCATION & DATE
VIENNA, AUSTRIA, 2002

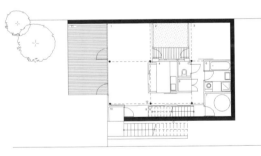

Ground floor

Section

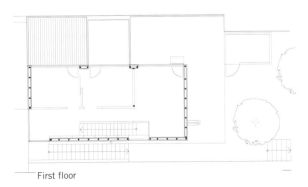

First floor

The two-story house was built on 540 square feet.

Inside, white combined with wood increases the light and feeling of space in a building that is much smaller than it seems.

018

A team of architects was responsible for this project, a single building with an articulated succession of spaces on five completely white levels. The commission represented certain difficulties because the young couple that owned the building had a large number of requirements.

Conceptually, the project made use of contemporary formulas to help define the different uses of the small space. The rooms were divided according to the activities that would take place in them and labeled 0 through 8. Some of the rooms were designed for use with the couple in mind, while taking into account the individuality and singularity of the residents. The intention of the architects was to explore the potential of the interior and part of this task consisted of making sure that no space followed hierarchical arrangement. In this way, they were able to achieve two basic goals: a richness of space, and volumes with pure lines.

On the outside, an object can be seen projecting from the fifth floor; it is the mast of the "Charity", a historic yacht built in 1896.

1098 SQUARE FEET

ARCHITECTS
HIROYUKI ARIMA + URBAN FOURTH

PHOTOGRAPHER
KOUJI OKAMOTO

LOCATION & DATE
KANAGAWA, JAPAN, 2003

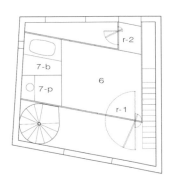

Floor plan

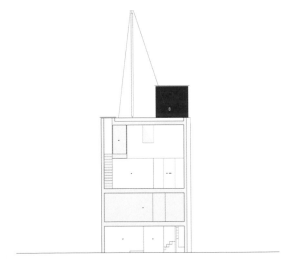

Section

5

An old mast from a yacht dating to 1896 crowns the fifth floor.

HOUSE IN SETAGAYA

This house is located in a residential area of the Setagaya Ward in the city of Tokyo. The building rises like an illuminated prism that at night fills the landscape with its size and dynamism. The rhythm created by alternating solid materials with translucent surfaces on the exterior corresponds to a very unique layout in the interior. In this sense, the bathroom is located on the terrace and becomes the most important room of the house. Its function goes beyond normal everyday use, becoming a lounging area where one can chat on sunny days while taking a nice bath.

The interior layout follows a line that divides the spaces according to their function, more open in the public settings and more closed in the private.

Furniture with simple, pure lines and no superfluous elements that would affect function and fluidity was chosen to ensure a free and light-filled space.

1141 SQUARE FEET

ARCHITECTS
NAYA ARCHITECTS: MANABU + ARATA

PHOTOGRAPHER
MAKOTO YOSHIDA

LOCATION & DATE
TOKYO, JAPAN, 2004

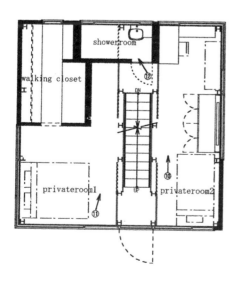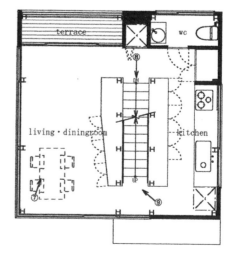

Floor plans

Each space is white and furnished simply.

ELLIOTT HOUSE

This project consisted of enlarging and renovating a small house, whose location on a very steep site determined the architecture of the new residence. Oblique and angled lines create the appearance of a distorted cube on the outside, in an interesting play of deceiving perspectives whose main function is to adapt the geometry of the house to the characteristics of the site. On the top floor, the window frames are angled parallel to the street, in a subtle reference to the slope of the ground.

The long panoramic windows that surround the top floor were designed as a response to the abundant vegetation in the area. Their views are mainly of the treetops, creating the sensation of being in a sophisticated tree house in some remote area of Canada or Scandinavia. The house combines a sensitive response to the context of the location with an innovative and contemporary architecture, making the residence a project that is worthy of mention.

1173 SQUARE FEET

ARCHITECTS
BERE:ARCHITECTS

PHOTOGRAPHER
PETER COOK/VIEW

LOCATION & DATE
LONDON, UNITED KINGDOM, 2004

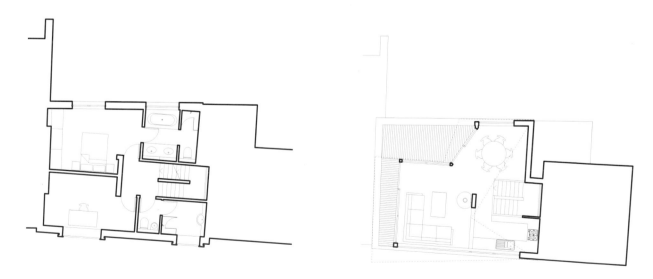

Floor plans

A Scandinavian fireplace dominates the top floor. Fresh air enters directly behind the glass panel, avoiding the heat loss typical of open fireplaces.

The interiors become especially dramatic thanks to the unusual architecture that makes use of fanciful perspectives.

THE LONG HOUSE

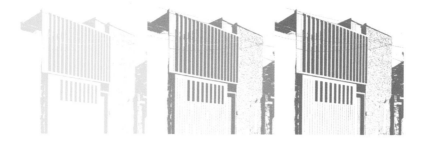

This residence, located in Percy Lane, was built in front of the garden of another house to take advantage of the empty space between the two buildings. The goal of Grafton Architects, the team responsible for the project, was to liberate and transform the narrow garden in order to take advantage of the elongated configuration of this natural setting.

Structurally, the overall design is defined by its elongated shape. A laminated wood structure at the front conceals and protects the geometry of the lines. This enclosure allows the natural light inside the building to be manipulated to create private spaces with more or less illumination. Inside, the house includes interesting elements that increase the feeling of spaciousness. On the main level is an open space that includes the living area, the dining room, a study, and the kitchen. The top floor on the other hand contains the most private areas, like the master bedroom. The resulting effect is one of architectural simplicity and austerity.

1184 SQUARE FEET

ARCHITECTS
GRAFTON ARCHITECTS

PHOTOGRAPHER
DENNIS GILBERT/VIEW

LOCATION & DATE
DUBLIN, IRELAND, 2001

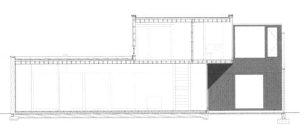

Section

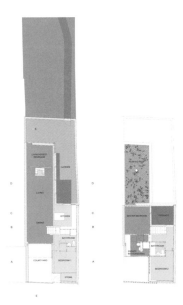

Floor plan

Light filters through the wooden screen and defines the level
of intimacy in each room.

The rooms have wood furniture pieces with straight and simple lines.

A spiral staircase connects the ∫building's three floors. The skylight in the ceiling allows natural light to flow into each room, making them appear more spacious.

KASSAI HOUSE

This house, located in one of the most expensive areas of Tezukayama, south of Osaka, is an example of the way in which some buildings in this area were subdivided to mitigate the high cost of construction.

The house is in the form of a cube, and is surrounded by a frame that seems to protect the residence that is concealed inside. The interior design was inspired by this cube-shaped main structure, which exhibits pure lines and a flat roof.

At the base, the entrance appears to support a facade that was constructed with exacting proportions. The house consists of two clearly defined levels, both of which have wood and steel as the dominant materials. The living area is full of light and appears larger than it really is.

The interior garden located in the rear directs the sunlight to the interior through a large window that separates this area from the private quarters. In the center is a slender fireplace that enhances the feeling of spaciousness as it rises up through the interior.

1249 SQUARE FEET

ARCHITECTS
KIYOSHI SEY TAKEYAMA + AMORPHE

PHOTOGRAPHER
KOICHI TORIMURA

LOCATION & DATE
OSAKA, JAPAN, 2003

The house consists of two different levels within a cube, which has clean lines and a flat roof.

In the middle of the living room a chimney rises up to the ceiling emphasizing the height of the small space.

NON-URBAN RESIDENCES

The willingness to rediscover small things is not always a choice dictated by limitations of size, since the small single-family homes that are found on the outskirts of urban centers and in the country do not face the problem of scarcity of space. These houses are the result of a personal quest and are one of the few ways in which home owners can experiment and also challenge the creative abilities of their architects. At the same time, they are the true reflection of the occupants' dream home.

The traditional house plan, where the common and private areas are clearly defined, gives way to new solutions for designing compact houses, where the approach makes the creation of new relationships between these two spaces possible. Flexible partitions and the design of multifunctional furniture, along with the creative use of a room's height and the extension of the interior space into the outdoors are some of the resources commonly used by the architects. This way they counteract the claustrophobic feeling that can be caused by small spaces.

Each of the 167 panels that make up the house consists of two boards glued together to make a 1 5/8 inch-thick unit.

In contrast with the living room's rectangular ceiling, the two bedroom cabins are defined by walls that mimic the exterior's oval shape.

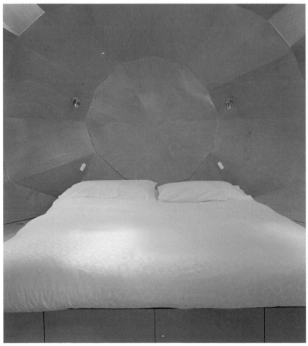

CLAUDIA BRUCKNER RESIDENCE

The color of the wood siding gives this project its other name, the Fire Red House, which was designed as a home for a woman, a cat, and a dog. The simplicity of the exterior reflects an equally simple layout inside, creating an atmosphere that is so closely tied to all the essential elements that its purity is almost poetic. An efficient organization of the interior makes the house feel much larger than its 750 square feet.

To maximize the space, the various areas inside were defined with different surface levels and ceiling heights, all within a single space, to take full advantage of each area. Furthermore, unequal lighting gives each room a personal character and differentiates it from the others. This design is very natural, which is reflected in its distribution as well as in the materials used, in an effort to make simplicity its main objective.

753 SQUARE FEET

ARCHITECT
HANS-PETER LANG

PHOTOGRAPHER
ALBRECHT SCHNABEL

LOCATION & DATE
RANKWEIL, AUSTRIA, 2001

Windows of very different shapes and sizes give the building a humorous quality.

The bedroom is located on the top floor at one end of the house, and the more public areas, such as the living room and the kitchen, are on the lower level.

The porch is open to magnificent surrounding views, providing a feeling of spaciousness inside the house.

Multifunctional areas were created to resolve the limitations presented by the space, such as this photo studio which has a compact kitchen/range.

The house consists of two levels and a gallery at the top, which can be reached by a stairway with floating steps.

SOL

With this design, the Austrian architecture studio Planhaus redefines the market for prefabricated single-family homes. Intelligently designed, economic, and flexible, the Sol model distinguishes itself from the competition by offering its customers an open floor plan.

The building consists of a compact wood structure, with clearly defined lines, and a flat roof. Large windows help create a bright space that is full of light and makes full use of passive solar energy. The outside of the structure is covered with narrow wood siding that was installed onsite, and the ecologically friendly material was also used in the interior of the house.

The Sol model, measured at 818 square feet, has two levels. The space is laid out around a central bathroom, which is the only fixed element. The rest of the plan permits a free distribution of space, which can be adapted to the needs of each client allowing them to come up with individual solutions while enjoying the economic advantages of mass production.

818 SQUARE FEET

ARCHITECTS
PLANHAUS

PHOTOGRAPHER
ANGELO KAUNAT

LOCATION & DATE
VIENNA, AUSTRIA, 2001

Practical and economical, the construction phase of the Sol model is short and the house can be ready for use in three months.

RUPP HOUSE

The contrast of wood, steel, and glass characterize this house, which is located on a site that is barely 1,055 square feet. The Rupp House is constructed of a steel frame with the actual house suspended within it, a wood box containing all the spaces – living room, kitchen, bathroom, and bedrooms – in a single, open volume. On the south side, a spacious terrace extends outwards from the residence. Below the main volume of the house is another box, constructed on the ground and covered with glass. This transparent receptacle contrasts with the hermetic wood facades and contains the garage.

A simple stairway also made of steel, leads from the garage to a long space on the west side of the house. This hallway, formed by the separation between the frame and the main building, leads to the terrace and functions as a porch. When the yellow awning is lowered, it acts as a second skin that protects the house from the sun and the wind, and makes the open areas of the house more intimate.

1055 SQUARE FEET

ARCHITECTS
ALEXANDER FRÜH, ALEXANDER FETZ

PHOTOGRAPHER
ADOLF BEREUTER

LOCATION & DATE
HARD, AUSTRIA, 2001

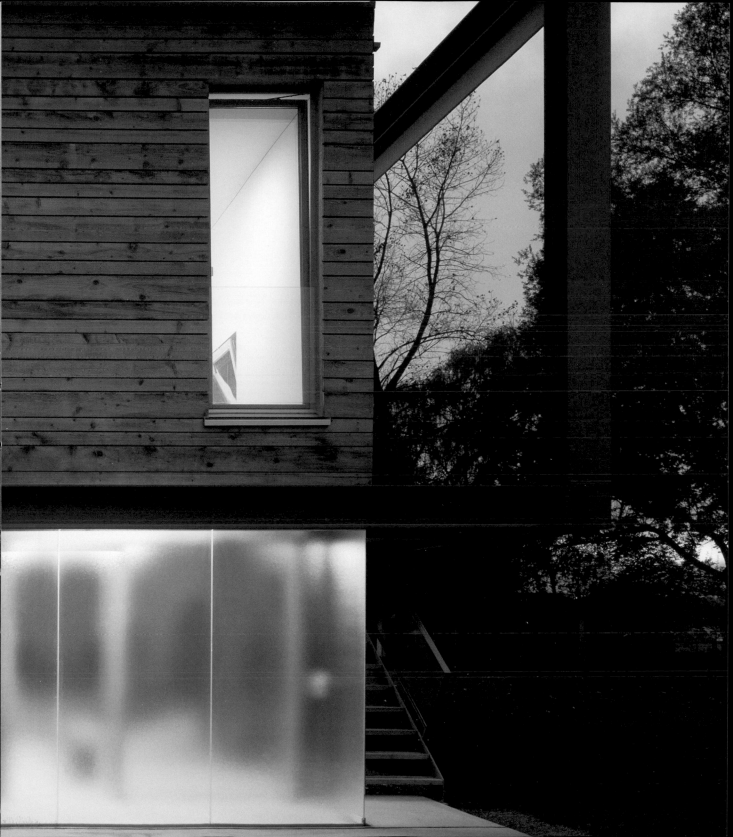

SINGLE-FAMILY HOME IN GAUSES

The structure of this single-family home was predetermined by the characteristics of the site, which was square, and the zoning ordinances that prohibited building more than one story. The architect took on this project intending to build a small house, as open as possible, resembling a large porch. He designed the walls as sliding doors that could be opened completely as a way to bring the outdoors inside. The siding plays and important role in achieving a transparency that makes the house feel like a porch.

The interior of the house is divided into three areas: on one side, the master bedroom, the dressing room, and one of the bathrooms, with an adjoining space earmarked for a study and reading area. On another, the living room and entrance to the home, placed in the center. And finally, an area for the kitchen/dining room and a small bedroom with its own bathroom, which are separated from the other rooms by a large sliding door.

1055 SQUARE FEET

ARCHITECT
ESTEVE TERRADES

PHOTOGRAPHER
JORDI CANOSA

LOCATION & DATE
GAUSES DE DALT, SPAIN, 2000

A ten foot separation from the sliding aluminum doors leaves room
for a possible future addition to the house.

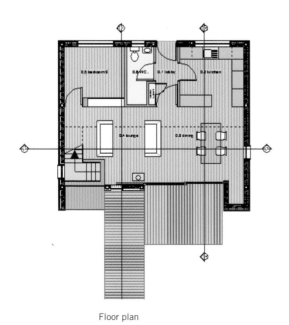

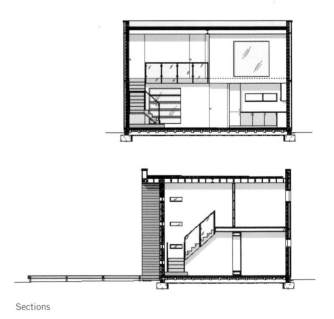

Floor plan

Sections

The common areas such as the dining room and the living room are located just inside the window wall and receive the most light.

The white walls and the furniture, which is also completely white, seem to enhance the effect of light emanating from the windows, which contrasts with the opacity of the exterior siding.

The glass siding in the living room, which open to the outside along the terrace, allows the house to receive abundant natural light.

The sense of solidity exuded by the upper facade contrasts with the transparency of the ground floor. The lack of privacy allows them to be used as common areas, while the bedrooms, on the other hand, are located on the top floor.

4X4 HOUSE

In Japan the dynamic rhythm of a contemporary global metropolis coexists with the conservative foundation of a traditional culture, resulting in a celebration of sophisticated contradictions. These elements, summed up in the juxtaposition of man and nature, establish the ideological principles that are the basis of the architecture of Tadao Ando.

The recipient of the Pritzker Prize for Architecture, among others, Ando designed a house within a four-story tower, whose square footprint, 4 x 4 meters, gave it its name. The most characteristic element is a cube with large windows that projects out from the top of the building, making room for the placement of a stairway. The ground floor houses the entrance, the bathroom and the sink. The second floor is reserved for the bedroom, and the third for the office, while the top floor holds the living area and the kitchen.

This design is the result of the willingness to transform the architectural space into a refuge for the spirit, an individual experience. This is, above all else, expressive architecture.

1270 SQUARE FEET

ARCHITECTS
TADAO ANDO ARCHITECT & ASSOCIATES

PHOTOGRAPHER
MITSUO MATSUOKA

LOCATION & DATE
HYOGO, JAPAN, 2003

Facing the shore of Awaji Island, the epicenter of the earthquake that devastated the island in 1995, the house is imbued with the memory of it.

The philosophical principle of building is omnipresent in Ando's work: the creative act defines a personal universe in which a person can identify, discover and define his or her own place.

SINGLE-FAMILY HOME
AND STUDIO

This project was commissioned by a couple of professionals who work in the fields of design and music production, and required a specific, yet not large space to be used as a work area. The ideal solution in terms of budget, architecture, and function for the long 75 x 290 foot site, located in a green belt on the outskirts of Berlin, was the construction of two separate buildings. The front part is the residence, while the rear of the building is used as a sound studio.

The residence consists of two floors: the design studio, living area, and kitchen are on the ground floor, and two bedrooms designed around a central hallway are upstairs on the second level. Wood plays and important role in the structure and finish of the house. The walls and ceiling inside are made of untreated wood, and stained larch boards are used on the outside walls. Openings in the walls with inset transparent materials such as polycarbonate and glass allow natural light into the rooms creating a bright and diaphanous interior.

1292 SQUARE FEET

ARCHITECTS
AUGUSTIN & FRANK ARCHITEKTEN

PHOTOGRAPHER
WERNER HUTHMACHER

LOCATION & DATE
FALKENSEE, GERMANY, 2003

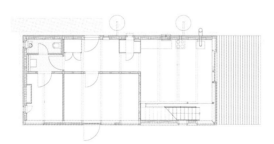

Ground floor

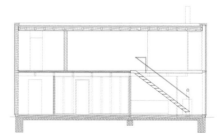

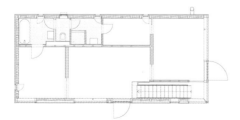

First floor

Sections

The glass facades of both buildings establish a visual communication, while direct access between the two is made possible through the sliding-glass doors.

ADDITIONS

Whether in the country or in the city, classic or modern in design and style, the aesthetics of an addition to a house is always affected by the relationship that is created between the new structure and the already existing one.

It may be designed as a guesthouse or an extension of an existing space such as the living room. In any case, the new addition is not created from thin air, and its appearance will always be influenced by its predecessor, the original dwelling. Interest lies in solutions that have been created to make the addition compatible with the original design. The addition will either attempt to seamlessly blend with the original building, or reject the style of the house to justify its existence as a completely different design. Innovative materials or materials borrowed from the vernacular tradition, along with the use of colors that create a feeling of space, are some of the most commonly used techniques in this section. However, it is the architectural relationship between the two parts of the house that is analyzed in this chapter.

Burying the structure in the ground allows the roof to be used as a bench or as a surface for any activity.

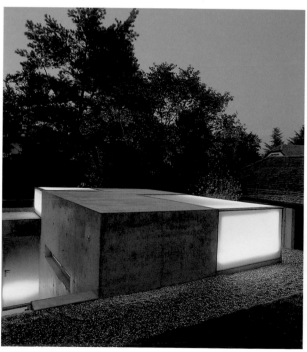

The outer layer of concrete was tinted a grayish green that complements the coloring of the windows.

REBUILDING OF HOUSE KÖNIG

This small addition to a residence is a separate building, independent from the main house. Despite the fact that the extension is connected to the house, the Austrian architects Peter and Ute Wimmer decided to give it a completely different treatment to visually separate the new space from the existing building. Although the most evident difference is the red color of its wood siding, contrasting with the white stone used in the main volume, the style of the new addition also strays considerably from its predecessor in the shape of its roof and the windows. The expansion exudes an air of contented modernity, and although it is contrary to the traditional Austrian style of the main residence, the two parts achieve a mutual balance.

In stylistic terms, even while proclaiming its own style, the project does not attempt to hide the fact that it forms part of a shared space, and that is exactly what creates the formal balance that this small 463 square foot space radiates.

463 SQUARE FEET

ARCHITECTS
ARCHITEKTURBÜRO WIMMER-ARMELLINI

PHOTOGRAPHER
IGNACIO MARTÍNEZ

LOCATION & DATE
LUSTENAU, AUSTRIA, 2003

The diagonals are also important in the interior, where they are used in ceilings of different heights. The shelves that cover one of the walls make the differences quite obvious.

264

The bedroom and a balcony are on the second floor. On the ground floor an atrium opens the space to the outside.

The glass facades and skylights give the house a feeling of spaciousness and light.

LEVIS HOUSE

Fluidity and formal restraint in the structure are the key elements of this house designed as an addition to a rural residence. The design concept, a joint effort of the UdA Studio and Davide Volpe, was a contemporary update of rural structures.

Its architectural design reveals not only the interior layout of the physical space, it enhances the beauty of the surrounding landscape as well. From the outside, a structure of frames made of fir wood encloses the building and adds verticality to the strong horizontals that are typical of country houses.

The Levis House was built in an old hay barn, with about 915 square feet on two floors connected by an exterior stairway. The kitchen, the bathroom, the dining room, and a bedroom are located on the main floor; and on the second floor are another bedroom, a living room, and a terrace. The architects refer to this building as "architectural language inspired in the joinery and assembly of horizontal and vertical planes".

The landscape pours into the interior like photographs seen through the screen of the wood frame and through the windows.

915 SQUARE FEET

ARCHITECTS
DAVIDE VOLPE AND UdA STUDIO

PHOTOGRAPHER
EMILIO CONTI

LOCATION & DATE
VANDORNO, ITALY, 1998

The screen of fir wood slats acts as a subtle filter that blurs the view of the house's structure.

Glass and stone, cleverly combined, create an architecturally
contemporary space in a predominantly traditional setting.

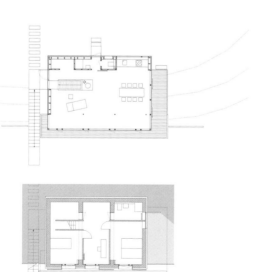

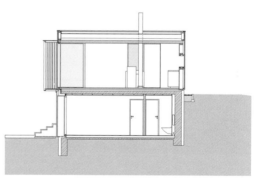

Section

Floor plans

The facade has wood screens, which shield the interior from the buildings surrounding the house.

TEMPORARY RETREATS

The projects studied in this section, designed as cabins, temporary residences, and vacation homes, spring from a common interest: the opportunity to get away from daily routines to enjoy the pleasures – as well as the austerity – of a different, simpler, and more human lifestyle. The challenges presented by some of the projects illustrated here, such as the lack of electricity, were sometimes a result of their extremely small size or their location. But they are not at odds with innovative architecture, or with design that is clever and aspiring to the highest esthetic standards. As in many fields where speculation often leads to formal experimentation, here different necessary functions are often combined because of the small size of many of these temporary residences, resulting in surprising solutions that often follow in the footsteps of vernacular tradition. The goal of this chapter is to examine the functional, technical, and aesthetic elements that have played a part in the creation of these vacation retreats, which are becoming increasingly popular.

The load-bearing walls were constructed with durable wood and then covered with wood siding.

The furniture is arranged facing the window walls; the bed, the kitchen table, and the chairs that define the space designated as the living area are aligned with the windows, which provide a magnificent view of the landscape.

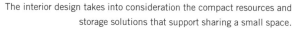

The interior design takes into consideration the compact resources and storage solutions that support sharing a small space.

All the walls are made of sheets of plywood covered with a layer of resin. A polystyrene panel inserted between the exterior and the interior plywood sheets provides effective insulation.

The structure uses tablet-like wood panels for windows that partially open the box.

The structure surrounding the stairs creates an analogy with the nearby trees, mimicking them in an attempt to integrate itself into the landscape.

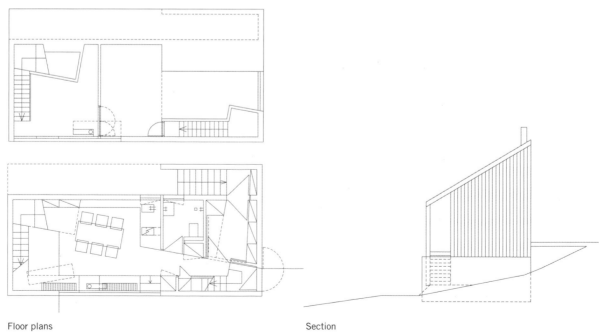

Floor plans

Section

The exterior surface combines wood, glass, and concrete in a simple architectural style with pure forms.

The climbing plants soften the structure's straight lines and visually connect the interior with the surroundings.

M-HOUSE

The M House is a framework with moveable parts that can undergo a wide range of aesthetic and functional changes. What at first glance seems to be an abstract and chaotic form is actually a simple and symmetrical structural base. This support consists of an assembly of rectangular steel tubes forming a square structure from which the surrounding panels unfold. They may be folded or opened at will, either vertically or horizontally. Some of them can be extended to create a covered outdoor area, like a terrace, or conversely, they can be brought inside and converted into part of the furniture, according to each person's needs.

The house, still under construction, is made of painted steel and Viroc, a relatively new fireproof product made from wood fiber in a cement base. Designed as a vacation home, guesthouse, or studio, the entire building is prefabricated and therefore can be disassembled for transporting.

1001 SQUARE FEET

ARCHITECT
MICHAEL JANTZEN

PHOTOGRAPHER
MICHAEL JANTZEN

LOCATION & DATE
GORMAN, TX, UNITED STATES, 2001

The furniture inside follows the logic of the exterior structure, based on steel panels, creating a geometric space highlighted by the green color of the panels.

The studio is located on the north side, whose wall is equipped with openings at the top and bottom that direct light across the surface of the floor.

The screen structure in front of the house allows diffused light to filter through during the brightest part of the day.

HOUSE IN CARRASCAL

The vastness of the Segovian landscapes of Carrascal was what influenced the choice of this town for the site of a small house that would serve as a weekend retreat, a place to escape the noise of the city and enjoy the solitude of the country. A clear and simple design was used for the structure, without flamboyant and superficially traditional themes, in order to focus attention on what is most important, that which, in the words of architect Mariano Martín, was "already there before we arrived". The landscape takes center stage in this project, to the extent that it determines the layout and the openings of the house.

The design of the building is based on two boxes, which were opened to the outside according to the desired views. The two structures – one small designed as a pavilion for guests and one large used as the main house – were located along an existing stone wall that turns at one end to create a private patio for the bedroom. The entrance to each of the boxes is reached from a solid stone step that is not attached to the building.

1184 SQUARE FEET

ARCHITECT
MARIANO MARTÍN

PHOTOGRAPHER
PEDRO LÓPEZ CAÑAS

LOCATION & DATE
CARRASCAL DE LA CUESTA, SPAIN, 2002

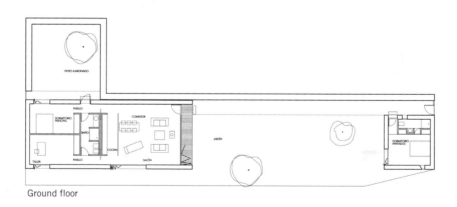

Ground floor

Elevation

Traditional materials from the area such as stucco with local sand and wood shutters made of Valsaín pine were used on the exterior.

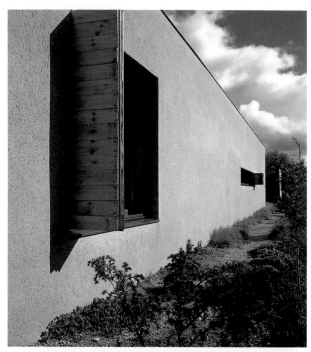

A gray, continuous floor of polished concrete covers
the surface of the entire house, which has no vertical elements except
for an opal glass wall that separates the living area from the kitchen and
acts as a reflective backdrop for the lights and shadows of the interior.

DIRECTORY

10 SLIT VILLA
tele-design
2-12-5 Openstudio Nope,
Mita Minatoku, Tokyo, Japan
T: +81 3 3769 0833
F: +81 3 3769 9893
www.tele-design.net
tele-web@tele-design.net

18 LAYER HOUSE
Hiroaki Ohtani
Chuo-ku, Osaka, Japan
T: +81 6 6203 2361
F: +81 6 6203 4277
www.nikken.co.jp
ootani@nikken.co.jp

26 TAVOLA
Milligram Studio Ltd.
4-2-17 Kugahara,
146-0085 Ota-ku,
Tokyo, Japan
T: +81 3 5700 8155
F: +81 3 5700 8156
www.milligram.ne.jp
info@milligram.ne.jp

32 PIXEL HOUSE
Slade Architecture
367 E 10th St
New York, NY 10009, USA
T: +1 212 677 6380
F: +1 212 677 6330
www.sladearch.com
james@sladearch.com

40 NATURAL WEDGE
Masaki Endoh/EDH
2-13-8 Honnmachi, Shibuyaku
151-0071 Tokyo, Japan
T: +81 3 3377 6293
F: +81 3 3377 6293
www.edh-web.com
edh-endoh@mvi.biglobe.ne.jp

48 WHITE RIBBING
Milligram Studio Ltd.
4-2-17 Kugahara,
146-0085 Ota-ku,
Tokyo, Japan
T: +81 3 5700 8155
F: +81 3 5700 8156
www.milligram.ne.jp
info@milligram.ne.jp

56 FOLD HOUSE
Cell Space Architects
3-12-3 Kugahara,
146-0085 Ohta-ku,
Tokyo, Japan
T: +81 3 5748 1011
F: +81 3 5748 1012
www.cell-space.com
mutsu@kt.rim.or.jp

64 ROOFTECTURE M
Shuhei Endo Architect
Institute
5-15-11, Nishitenma Kita-ku,
530-0047 Osaka, Japan
T: +81 6 6312 7455
F: +81 6 6312 7456
www.paramodern.com
endo@paramodern.com

72 HAUS P
Thaler.Thaler Architekten
Halbgasse 6/9
1070 Vienna, Austria
T: +43 1 526 81 42
F: +43 1 526 81 42
mail@thalerthaler.at

80 OI8
Hiroyuki Arima + Urban Fourth
95-1 57 Goshogadani Chuo-ku
Fukuoka
810-0027 Japan
T: +81-92-531-3236
F: +81-92-531-4251
yakkko76@rose.ocn.ne.jp

88 HOUSE IN SETAGAYA
NAYA Architects:
Manabu + Arata
2-1376-1F Kamimaruko
San-nocho, Nakahara-ku
211-0002 Kawasaki, Japan
T: +81 44 411 7934
F: +81 44 411 7935
www.f2.dion.ne.jp/-m-a.naya/
m-a.naya@f2.dion.ne.jp

94 ELLIOTT HOUSE
Bere:Architects
24 Rosebery Avenue,
London EC1R 4SX,
United Kingdom
T: +44 0 20 7837 9333
F: +44 0 20 7837 9444
www.bere.co.uk
jbere@bere.co.uk

102 THE LONG HOUSE
Grafton Architects
12 Dame Court,
Dublin 2, Ireland
T: +353 1671 3365
F: +353 1671 3178
info@graftonarchitects.ie

110 HOUSE IN MOTOAZABU
Cell Space Architects
3-12-3 Kugahara Ohta-ku
146-0085 Tokyo, Japan
T: +81 3 5748 1011
F: +81 3 5748 1012
www.cell-space.com
mutsu@kt.rim.or.jp

118 KASSAI HOUSE
Kiyoshi Sey Takeyama +
Amorphe
6F 215 Okura-cho,
Karasuma
Dori Takeya-machi
Agaru Nakagyo-ku,
604-0861 Kyoto, Japan
T: +81 75 256 9600
F: +81 75 256 9511
www.amorphe.jp
info@amorphe.jp

128 M7 PROTOTYPE
Cooperativa uro1.org
José Ramón Gutiérrez 282, 2°
832-0162 Santiago, Chile
T: +56 639 3389
www.uro1.org

136 COCOON HOUSE
Bellemo & Cat
4/358 Lonsdale Street,
Melbourne 3000, Australia
T: +61 967 000 39
F: +61 967 000 97
bellemocat@bigpond.com

146 CLAUDIA BRUCKNER
RESIDENCE
Hans-Peter Lang
Kustergasse 14b
A-6811 Göfis, Austria
T: +43 5522 76519
www.coa.at
lang@coa.at

154 MINIMAL HOUSE
Ivan Kroupa
Goncarenkova 10,
Prague 4, Czech Republic
T: +420 775 106 816
F: +420 244 460 103
www.ivankroupa.cz
ivankroupa@ivankroupa.cz

162 A HOUSE IN THE GARDEN
Archteam
Weyrova 3,
547 01 Nachod,
Czech Republic
T: +420 491 422 009
F: +420 491 422 009
www.archteam.cz
archteam@archteam.cz

170 SOL
Planhaus
Hollandstrasse 8/2,
A-1020 Vienna, Austria
T: +43 1 726 73 71
F: +43 1 726 73 10
www.planhaus.at
gt@planhaus.at

176 RUPP HOUSE
Früh Architekturbüro
Lochbachstrasse 6,
A-6971 Hard, Austria
T: +43 5574 77 447
F: +43 5574 77 410
www.frueh.at
office@frueh.at

184 SINGLE-FAMILY
HOME IN GAUSES
Esteve Terrades
Manuel Girona 75,
08034 Barcelona, Spain
T. +34 932 048 066
F. +34 932 804 721
www.arquitectes.coac.net/te-
rradasarquitectes
arqtes_terradas@coac.es

192 WESTLAKE HOUSE
Spacelab UK
Unit 404 Kings Wharf,
301 Kingsland Road,
E8 4DS London, UK
T: +44 20 7684 5392
F: +44 20 7684 5393
www.spacelabuk.com
info@spacelabuk.com

200 OPEN TO THE RIVER
Lacoste + Stevenson
Architects
301/85 William Street,
East Sydney 2011, Australia
T: +61 9360 8633
F: +61 9380 6231
www.lacoste-stevenson.com.au
david@lacoste-
stevenson.com.au

210 MISONOU HOUSE
Suppose Design Office
Makoto Tanijiri 730-0812,
13-2-3F Kako-machi Naka-ku,
Hiroshima, Japan
T. +81 82 247 1152
F. +81 82 247 1152
www.suppose.jp
info@suppose.jp

218 4x4 HOUSE
Tadao Ando Architect &
Associates
5-23 Toyosaki 2,
Chome Kita-ku,
531-0072 Osaka, Japan
T. +81 6 6375 1148
F. +81 6 6374 6240
taaa@mx6.nisiq.net

226 SINGLE-FAMILY
HOUSE AND STUDIO
Augustin & Frank Architekten
Schlesische Strasse 29-30,
10997 Berlin, Germany
T. +49 612 843 57
F. +49 612 843 59
augustin_und_frank@t-online.de

236 HOUSE IN VANDOEUVRES
Charles Pictet Architect
13 rue du Roveray,
1207 Geneva, Switzerland
T: +41 22 700 51 35
F: +41 22 700 51 07
www.pictet-architecte.ch
info@pictet-architecte.ch

244 REBUILDING
OF HOUSE KÖNIG
Architekturbüro Wimmer-
Armellini
Reichsstrasse 5,
6900 Bregenz, Austria
T: +43 5574 542420
F: +43 5574 542413
www.arching.at/wimmer-armellini
wimmer_armellini@vol.at

250 DONG HEON RESIDENCE
Seung H-Sang/Iroje Architects
& Planners
2-8 Dongsung-dong, Jongro-gu
110-809 Seoul, Korea
T: +82 2 763 2010
F: +82 2 745 3606
www.iroje.com
master@iroje.com

258 2PARTS HOUSE
Black Kosloff Knott Architects
Total House Level 9/180,
Russell St,
Melbourne 3000, Australia
T: +613 9671 4555
F: +613 9671 4666
www.b-k-k.com.au
office@b-k-k.com.au

266 SOLAR BOX
Driendl Architects
Mariahilferstrasse 9,
1060 Vienna, Austria
T: +43 15851868
F: +43 15851869
www.driendl.at
architekt@driendl.at

274 LEVIS HOUSE
UdA Studio
Via Valprato 68,
10155 Turin, Italy
T. +39 11 2489 489
F. +39 11 2487 591
www.uda.it
uda@uda.it

282 BETIKOA
F-451 Arquitectura
Caspe 35 entlo 1°
08010 Barcelona, Spain
T: +34 933 175 819
F: +34 933 175 819
F451@coac.net

290 ZENZMAIER HOUSE
Maria Flöckner und
Hermann Schnöll
Lasserstrasse 6a
A-5020 Salzburg, Austria
T: +43 662 878799
F: +43 662 878799
www.floecknerschnoell.com
atelier@floecknerschnoell.com

298 STUDIO AND GUESTHOUSE
GROSSENSEE
Loosen, Rüschoff + Winkler
Klopstockplatz 9
22765 Hamburg, Germany
T: +49 40 85 79 60
F: +49 40 85 60 93
www.lrw-architekten.de
mail@lrw-architekten.de

308 ZIG ZAG CABIN
Drew Heath
T: +61 414 491270
drewheath@ozemail.com.au

316 WEE HOUSE
Geoffrey Warner/Alchemy
Architects
550 Vandalia St 314
St. Paul, MN 55114, USA
T: +1 651 647 6650
F: +1 651 647 6633
www.weehouses.com
info@weehouses.com

324 BOATHOUSE
Drew Heath
T: +61 414 491270
drewheath@ozemail.com.au

332 SUMMER CONTAINER
Markku Hedman
Menninkäisentie 5 C,
FI-02110 Espoo, Finland
T: +358 9 4555 180
F: +358 9 4555 181
markku.hedman@hut.fi

338 BOX HOUSE
Nicholas Murcutt/Neeson
Murcutt Architects
Level 5, 71 York St,
2000 Sydney, Australia
T: +61 2 8297 3590
F: +61 2 8297 3510
www.rneeson@iprimus.com.au
nmurcutt@iprimus.com.au

346 KEENAN TOWER HOUSE
Marlon Blackwell
100 West Center Street,
Suite 001,Fayetteville,
Arkansas 72701, USA
T: +1 479 973 9121
F: +1 479 251 8281
www.marlonblackwell.com/
info@marlonblackwell.com

354 SNOWBOARDERS COTTAGE
Ivan Kroupa
Goncarenkova 10,
Prague 4, Czech Republic
T: +420 775 106 816
F: +420 244 460 103
www.ivankroupa.cz
ivankroupa@ivankroupa.cz

362 CLARABOYA HOUSE
Flemming Skude
Aabenraa 33,
DK 1124 Copenhagen K,
Denmark
T: +45 3332 6746
F: +45 3268 6822
flemming.skude@karch.dk

370 HOLIDAY HOME SEEWALD
Marte.Marte Architekten
Totengasse 18,
6833 Weiler, Austria
T: +43 5523 52587
F: +43 5523 52587 9
architekten@marte-marte.com

378 SUMMERHOUSE IN DYNGBY
Claus Hermansen
Filmbyen 23,
DK 8000 Århus, Denmark
T: +45 8734 0755
F: +45 8734 1855
www.lplush.dk
info@lplush.dk

380 M HOUSE
Michael Jantzen
27800 North McBean
Parkway, Suite 319,
Valencia, CA 91354, USA
T: +1 310 989 1897
www.humanshelter.org
mjantzen@yahoo.com

394 SUMMER HOUSE
Henning Larsens Tegnestue
Vesterbrogade 76,
DK 1620, Copenhagen,
Denmark
T: +45 8233 3000
F: +45 8233 3099
www.hlt.dk
hlt@hlt.dk

400 HOUSE AT JUQUEHY
Alvaro Puntoni
Artur de Azevedo 32, 7
São Paulo 05404 000, Brazil
T: +55 11 3062 1941
www.puntoni.arq.br
alvaro@puntoni.arq.br

408 HOUSE IN CARRASCAL
Mariano Martín
Rafael Salazar Alonso 2 4º,
28007 Madrid, Spain
T: +34 915 730 564
F: +34 915 730 564
www.marianomartin.com
estudio@marianomartin.com